The Outdoor Facilitator's Handbook

Curt Davidson

To. my friend
Noah,

It was a great time working
our first course at Odin together.
You are a great instructor. Keep
caring for students & you will
touch many lives. I look forward
to many trails & stories in the
coming years.

Yours,

Go For Broke Publications

For distribution information please contact Curt Davidson at cubdavid@indiana.edu

Table of Contents

To learn more and continue the discussion, find the Outdoor Facilitator's Hangout on Facebook.

How to use this guide

As there has been an increasing trend in the use of adventure experiences for reaching a wide range of recreational, educational, developmental, and therapeutic goals, sound facilitation methods and techniques have become essential for outdoor educators. Facilitation in outdoor adventure learning is an art that incorporates a wide range of disciplines, from social and psychological sciences to physical and nature therapies. Success in facilitation also requires a sincere interest in helping others attain their best, and a willingness to be accommodating and empathetic in addressing individual needs as well as group dynamics.

It takes time and experience to build one's skill as a facilitator, and no book or manual can substitute for experience with groups in the field. While a climbing guide will get you to the climbing site and provide specific clues about the route, it is not intended to tell you how to specifically climb the route. The intention of this book is not to provide an all-inclusive guide to theories and techniques of facilitation. But it will get you started with different discussions, and should be used as a reference tool to instigate certain approaches or fall back on when you need ideas or want to mix up your group discussions.

As you will see, there are no absolute rules to facilitation and a flexible style and wide range of ability will help you cater to the majority of your students. Remember that no debrief is perfect, and the best we can do is vary the styles we use to target each student at some point during the course.

Facilitation Defined: Facilitation—"to make easier"—is the art of being able to condition your students to better understand their activities in relation to their outcomes, and to plant seeds in their minds about specific learnings they can glean from a particular experience. A skilled facilitator will help students draw out these learnings through activities, followed by connections in the process of exploring and discovering how they might utilize those learnings in their future lives.

So the goal of facilitation is to connect experiences with *learnings* intended to help a person or group in future events, and with life in general.

As facilitators, we need to learn specific ways to apply the "what, so what, and now what" which is the conventional method for facilitation. There are many types of facilitation, but the main focus of this book is to select techniques that are appropriate for facilitating experiences in an outdoor setting for certain groups and individuals. It is important to consider which outcomes you need to focus on. High-functioning groups achieve more goals and are generally more capable of maximizing their experience. As a facilitator, you will want to focus some of your attention on enhancing the level at which your group is performing. This includes deeper concepts such as communication, trust, and decision making, not simply "teambuilding." As your groups are usually formed on a temporary basis, you may want to facilitate for individual development, including concepts such as personal self-care, responsibility, connection to nature, and increasing self-confidence. Additional outcomes are explored later in this guide.

There are generally three levels at which instructors can facilitate, shown in Figure 1. Keep in mind that as you move upward, each level involves more challenging facilitation. Positive change in our students should be our goal, while the first step in that process is increasing awareness. Becoming aware is often enough to bring about change at some point in our students' activities and lives, but as facilitators, we won't always see the fruits of our labors.

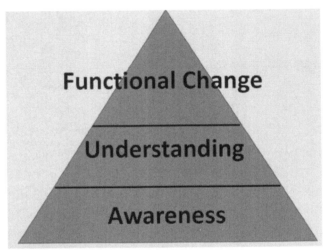

Figure 1: Depths of Facilitation
This figure illustrates the different depths of facilitation within individuals. As the facilitator, think about how

you could move students sequentially through this process.

- First, call attention to a problem or area for growth.
- Second, help them understand the issue, as well as strategies for improving upon it.
- Third, help facilitate change within themselves and facilitate opportunities for practicing and provide feedback for the student.

Functional change in our students' daily lives is usually our end goal for this process. Furthermore, consider each level as fundamentally important to the one above it. In other words, you cannot achieve change without being aware of a problem within yourself, and understanding exactly what that problem entails. For example, a student cannot improve their ability to communicate with others unless they are aware that they lack that skill, as well as understanding strategies for developing that ability.

The Facilitation Flow Model

This tool is designed to help you think through the debriefing process. Use it to organize your thoughts and think through the different debriefing considerations, and to keep your debrief headed in the right direction. It should also be useful to plan your debrief, and ensure you are mixing up the styles you are using. An explanation of each component will follow in later sections.

Facilitation Flow Model

Before

Outcomes pg 8
What outcomes should my students be getting from this experience?

Timing pg 15
Would it be best to debrief right after this activity or let the students process for awhile?

Learning Styles pg 11
What learning styles do I need to cater to during this debrief?

Setting pg 16
Where is the best setting for this that is free from distractions?

During

T - Trigger
R – Recall/Remember
A – Affect/Effect
C - Connection
T - Transference
pg 18

Dynamic Debriefing pg 22
90/10 Rule
Active Listening
Avoid Judgments
Ask follow-up Questions
Take notes

Closing

Closing pg 25
Use a quote or summation to provide a definitive ending or closing on an experience or debrief

Booster pg 26
Consider creating a booster or tangible ways to help the students remember the learning after the experience

Figure 2: This model is designed to help the facilitator think through planning and implementing of a debrief. Consider consulting it to add variety and flow to your discussions.

What Facilitation Can and Cannot Do

While it is tempting to think that as facilitators we have the ability to fix problems and change the lives of our students, the reality is this is a difficult and sometimes impossible task. You should be realistic as to what facilitation generally can and cannot accomplish, as outlined in this list of possibilities:

Can:
- Introduce new ideas
- Bring awareness
- Bubble issues to the surface
- Give opportunities for accomplishment
- Give opportunities for problem-solving

Cannot:
- Fix problems
- Make a perfect team
- Allow time for practice and development
- Change deep-seated personality traits
- Ensure a singular or perfect course

You should also consider the implications for yourself as a facilitator. Some groups are oftentimes unfixable, as in the case of scapegoating, when the group blames one member for all their problems, or in the case of personality clashes that prevent meaningful exchange. Additionally, some groups goals never seem to align with program or facilitators goals, often making for a bumpy course where your goals for the students never fully get realized.

More specifically, sometimes groups never reach their full potential or perform as highly as other groups you may have had. If this is the case, remember not to take all the responsibility, but examine what you may have done to not avoid the problem. These are difficult problems, and although you can call awareness to the situation, facilitators often can't remedy it due to outside circumstances or those beyond your control.

Outcomes of Facilitation

As facilitators, we often have ideas about what we believe our students *should* be learning from an experience. We may steer a group that has been rock climbing for a day toward a conversation about communication because it seems like a natural, purposeful outcome. This kind of debrief is referred to as "prescribed" because the facilitator is proposing the desired outcomes. Alternatively, the facilitator could go into a debrief with no agenda pertaining to the outcomes the students should be focused on. This allows the students to focus in on what was obvious to *them*, making this type of debrief the "discovery" method. Both of these methods have their advantages and disadvantages, as outlined below.

Discovery method

Allowing the students to discover themes about what they have learned from an experience has distinct advantages. Research shows that if students come up with ideas or themes on their own, they are more likely to remember them. Additionally, students may learn things that are extremely pertinent to their group or where they are at that moment. Not being a member of their group, facilitators may not know what some of these themes would be.

On the contrary, a facilitator may know what the group needs in order to become higher functioning, and the group may not discover the theme that the facilitator desires without coaching. An additional disadvantage to the discovery method is that it is difficult to get groups to have a meaningful discussion when they are a newly formed group. Furthermore, some groups may be more reluctant to discuss deeper or member-specific themes (e.g., in all-male groups, where themes may be explored from a gender perspective).

Prescribed method

Going into a debrief with preconceived themes is an alternative to the discovery method. This method is useful to utilize with new groups, to help set the stage for what type of themes and outcomes you would like the group to be gleaning from their experiences. It is also useful if you have identified an area for development for the group and would like to further their performance in that area. This is a great way to advance the goals of your program and participants. For example, if your program strongly values integrity, this would be a great theme with which to frame an activity, or to focus on during your debrief (more on framing below).

Prescribed debriefing also has its disadvantages. As stated above, students are less likely to personally connect and transfer themes or outcomes that the facilitator has generated. Additionally, prescribing themes can make debrief and activities feel contrived or scripted.

Below is a list of common outcomes that outdoor facilitators encounter or strive for on courses and debriefs. Remember that this list is a sample of potential outcomes in areas such as skill, character or insight development, not a comprehensive list. Students never cease to amaze as they share their new and creative insights:

- Self-Confidence
- Social Support
- Inspiration

- Integrity/Trust
- Leadership Skills
- Connection to Self

- Connection to Others
- Connection to Nature
- Time Management

- Sense of Belonging
- Enhanced Communication
- Increased Physical Ability

- Sense of Accomplishment
- Enhanced Decision Making
- Enhanced Compassion

- Integrity
- Inclusion
- Excellence

- Enjoyment/Fun
- Resilience
- Sense of Place

- Self-Awareness
- Social Competence
- Increased flexibility

- Autonomy
- Group Performance
- Risk management skills

- Locus of Control
- Enhanced Cooperation
- Maturity
- Hardiness

Discovering and Prescribing

The best method is often a blend of each style. For example, I may go into a debrief with a certain set of expected outcomes that I have commonly seen students glean from a specific experience (see the "Anticipated Outcomes" section, p 9). After initiating the discussion with a trigger (more on triggers to follow), I listen for students to connect the discussion to a larger theme or outcome that can be transferred back to their life. If they are failing to consider the greater outcomes that are prevalent, I may suggest outcomes I have brainstormed prior to the debrief through probing questions. This may help the students make connections to larger outcomes.

If you need to influence the students' discovery of their own outcomes, remember to guide the discussion with exploratory questions as opposed to lecturing them about what outcomes you have in mind. For example, instead of telling them they should trust each other after belaying one another on a climb, you might ask them, "Does anybody have any insights into the issue of trust amongst group members after rock climbing today?"

Learning and Processing Styles

It is best to vary your techniques, such as in prescribed and discovery methods, because students possess various learning styles. According to current theories, people are generally seen as either external or internal processors. Internal processors typically draw meaning from an activity internally, while in solitude or journaling. External processors will typically draw meaning from an experience while discussing it in a group. External processors generally thrive in either large or small groups. As facilitators, it is therefore critical that we take this into consideration when structuring our debriefs.

It is important to cater to as many learning styles as often as we can, to increase our potency while facilitating discussions and trying to maximize learning and transference.

When facilitating a discussion, it is crucial to remember that sitting around in a circle is basically catering to people who are external processors (who learn by talking). Traditionally this has been the most common way to debrief after activities have occurred. But we now know that only about half the students in any group will effectively learn in this manner. The debrief of a climbing day, for example, might lend itself to the traditional method of sitting around in a circle talking about what the students have learned. But to add variety, and to cater to group members who tend to process internally, after a day of rappelling, you could break the group into three smaller groups and give them questions to discuss in these groups. This would allow people who process best in small groups to thrive during a discussion.

When mixing up your methods to meet the greatest variety of learning and processing styles, special consideration should thus be given for students who process experiences internally, or who thrive in debriefs while they are processing alone. Avoid pressing anyone to speak in a group setting, and be sure to not judge "quieter" participants as inadequate in any way, and to encourage them to use the communication method most suited to their needs in a style that is suggestive and empathetic, not dogmatic. To capitalize on this more passive learning style, you may want to simply provide quiet time for reflection after an experience. Furthermore, you could provide some prompts for them to think about or reflect upon to make sure you are still providing some structure for their time.

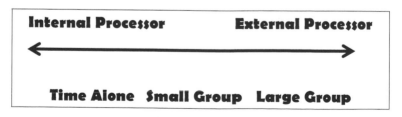

Figure 3: Spectrum of processing styles and techniques

Framing

Framing is a technique that often gets used whether we as instructors recognize it or not. In essence, framing is setting up an activity with the intention of preparing the students for a specific learning outcome which occurs in the setup of the activity. With framing, it is implicit that you are *prescribing* the outcomes that your students will glean from the upcoming experience. For example:

> If you want a group to think about setting goals, you may frame and brief an activity using the word "goal" several times. After the activity, you would then steer your discussion around how the group members set and meet goals for themselves. This can be an effective way to address group or personal needs without being judgmental of the group or individuals.

As a facilitator, you may choose to "frame" an activity for students about what to expect, or what you want them to glean from an experience. This builds off the foundation of facilitating with preconceived themes in mind. For example:

> You may tell each student to choose a rock to pick up and carry that represents a burden each of them feels they carry with them. After carrying it up to a rappel site, students announce to the group what the rock represents before they rappel off the edge.

They leave the rock on top of the ledge to symbolize leaving their burdens behind.

Framing is helpful in ensuring that your students are thinking on a deeper level than, "This is a cool activity." It is also a useful way to set the stage up for a meaningful discussion after an activity. Yet like any preconceived themes, framing may limit what your students may naturally glean from an experience. But used correctly, it can enhance and enrich an experience.

Timing

Timing is an important component of debriefing. There are a variety of factors to consider when planning the time to debrief and for how long. Remember that the average adult can focus their attention for only eight minutes, so your debriefs should take this into consideration. Don't be afraid to end a debrief if a topic has become exhausted or the students begin to repeat each other. Conversely, don't be afraid to draw out a debrief if there is a meaning that the students are missing out on. Utilize the "pregnant pause" whenever possible. This technique allows for other people who are hesitant to chime in. For example:

Sit silent for about eight seconds to provide an opportunity for reluctant people to speak up. This is also a great way to ensure no one else has anything they would like to contribute before you provide closing remarks.

While deciding when to debrief, it is also important to consider how much time has elapsed since the activity. Keep in mind it may be appropriate to debrief during or directly after an activity. These discussions are usually emotionally charged and allow for the students to talk through their learning as it is happening. This method naturally caters to extroverts and students who are quick to process things. Emotions and strong visual stimulus will likely play a large factor in when you want to debrief. For example:

> Seeing a rapid that a student just successfully ran might lend itself to a powerful debrief while you're still in sight of the rapid. Conversely, a group conflict, which should be resolved in a timely manner, might be an instance to delay the debrief and allow tempers to cool.

Just as we vary our methods, we should vary our timeliness in debriefs. To meet the needs of introverts, or for students who need more time to gather their thoughts, you may want to wait until the evening or even the next morning to debrief a day or activity. This allows the students to gather their thoughts and reflect on their own about an experience. These discussions usually have more depth and less emotion. Additionally, students aren't fatigued from just completing an activity and may have more energy to invest in a discussion.

Again, each method has many pros and cons depending on circumstances, and the wise facilitator will vary their styles to cater to different learning styles and speeds at which your students process an experience.

Setting

Choosing the location of your debrief is as important as choosing the timing. Remember these important factors which can greatly influence your debrief:

Provide comfort – Choose a location where they will be comfortable and can focus for the length of time you have planned for your debrief.

Eliminate distractions – Face the students away from visual or noise distractions, or move away from them altogether. For example, the ocean is a huge distraction, so make sure the students face away from it.

Time of day – Consider whether the time is conducive to having an in-depth discussion, as in, is it about to rain or get dark? Additionally, consider the energy level of the group so you don't have students falling asleep during the discussion (people are generally sleepy after meals, for example, or in late afternoon).

Provide an interesting venue – Students will appreciate a designated "special spot" to have evening debriefs. This can also be helpful in developing a consistent culture and setting for your debriefs.

Activity specific location - If the students may benefit from debriefing where an activity took place, consider choosing a location where that site is still visible (i.e. a mountain they climbed earlier that day).

Safe Environment – Facilitate a safe atmosphere in which the students know they can share sensitive information. A good way to do this is to share something quite personal about yourself that you are comfortable to share, thus setting up the environment to be a time for vulnerability and a safe place for expressing that. For example, a facilitator might consider sharing something like not being an effective communicator and being inadequate at sharing feelings. This approach also sets the expectation that these facilitations will be more in-depth than discussing what the students liked about the day.

TRACT

In facilitation's most basic form, the acronym TRACT – trigger, recall/remember, affect/effect, connection and transference – provides a general framework for thinking about how we might debrief an experience. Utilizing TRACT can help you transition through the debrief experience and also help your students "rationalize" through processing an experience.

Trigger: Triggers are activities or prompts to help the students start the process of thinking about what they learned from an activity. Use a trigger to help initialize a conversation about a particular experience.

Recall/Remember: Use the trigger or further questioning to help students remember what happened to them during an activity on many levels, physically, socially and emotionally.

Affect/Effect: Affect is the emotional impact that an experience has on the student, and the effect is its end product. For example, feeling frustrated (affect) and expressing that frustration to the group (effect) would be the affect/effect of an experience. Facilitate the discussion with follow-up questions about what affect/effects occurred during their experience. Encourage the students to use "I" statements during this section to help them "own" their commentary in relation to specific, individual responses.

Connection: Dig deeper with the students and ask them to connect the specific examples they are using to broader outcomes that may be more relevant to their everyday lives (more on outcomes below).

Transference: This is the final and most important step, when you facilitate the students' connection to the themes and outcomes previously discussed, and how they might affect their everyday lives *when they're back in their normal settings (school, work, home life, etc.)*

Triggers

Triggers are prompts or cues we can use to get discussions started and to lead them in a positive direction. Again, it is important to utilize a variety of triggers to keep things interesting as well as make these discussions fun. Triggers can be a great way to help your students connect things in nature to their experience, as well as help them express their thoughts and what they have learned. Here is a list of triggers to help get the debrief process started:

1. <u>Highs/lows (roses and thorns)</u>: Have the students state their high point and low points for the day;

2. <u>Symbolic Representation</u>: Have your students find an object in nature that represents their day or learning and explain why they chose that object;

3. <u>Scaling</u>: Choose a theme or several themes and have the group rate themselves or their group performance on a scale. Follow up with why they gave themselves, or the group, that number and what they could do to get to a more desirable number;

4. <u>Writing</u>: Choose a writing exercise, such as a poem or personal letter, for the students to write that expresses learnings or feelings they experienced during the activity;

5. <u>3-2-1</u>: Think of a sequence of things that build upon each other that you can ask your students about for the day. For example, 3-things you learned, 2-how it connects to yourself or group, 1-implications that learning has for their future;

6. <u>Mini-Solo</u>: Have the students take 2-30 minutes to quietly reflect about an activity;

7. <u>Partner Interview</u>: Break the students off in pairs and have them interview each other about their experience and what they learned. Combining this with walking works particularly well with male students;

8. <u>Anonymous Circle</u>: Have the group stand in a circle with one person in the middle. State themes such as "Made you smile today" and have the person in the middle touch people in the back who the theme applies to;

9. <u>Metaphoric Representation</u>: Ask the group to draw specific connections between the activity and themes. For example, you may ask a group, "What could the climbing rope represent in our group?" This may illicit a response such as, "It represented for me the connection and trust our group must have to accomplish our goals";

10. <u>Phone Call</u>: Ask the group what they would tell their parents or friends about their day or activity if they could call them at the time. Follow up with the question, "what if the parent or friend asked, 'What's the point of that activity?'";

11. <u>Natural Artscape</u>: Have the students draw a picture in the sand or dirt, or have them sculpt a

scene using natural objects such as sticks or rocks that represent the experience for them. Have them describe their methods and ask follow-up questions. Remember Leave No Trace principles (return materials to natural place) when using this method;

12. <u>Group Skit</u>: Have the group act out a skit depicting their experience. This is usually a nice way to end a course or debrief an experience that the instructors were not present for such as final expedition;

13. <u>Mountains Speak for Themselves</u>: Remember that you do not always have to debrief if the group is burnt out, or not in the mood. This is commonly known as the "mountains speak for themselves" method;

Write in other triggers you've found useful:

14._____

15._____

16._____

17._____

Dynamic Debriefing

Debriefing can be closely compared to the way journalists interview. This is a funny way to think about debriefing, but if you have ever watched Oprah, or heard Ira Glass on *This American Life*, it's pretty obvious that their success comes from their ability to draw out information from their guests by asking probing questions. Here are a few things that great facilitators focus on:

90/10 rule – Facilitators should only talk 10 percent of the time while the students talk 90 percent of the time;

Active Listening – Make eye contact, and summarize what you heard from the students;

Avoid Judgments – Never judge what a person or group says or does. Instead, try to get them to come to their own conclusions about what happened and how they should express their experiences;

Follow-up Questions – Ask follow-up questions to get the students to specify what they mean, how it applies to them, or what their feelings were about a particular event;

Avoid Yes/No Questions – Questions which allow one-word, yes or no answers are generally a poor way to facilitate. They also require the facilitator to ask follow-up questions. Start with an open-ended question;

Note Taking – Don't be afraid to take notes about what students say so you can bring up recurring themes, issues that they fail to address, or your thoughts on how to help facilitate the discussion. But you may want to be up front about note-taking and ask for their permission first.

Transference

Transference is the application of a skill, technique, or method that a student learns on their outdoor program, to their life back at home in their "normal" setting. Considered one of the most important components of the adventure education model, it is often the entire reason many of us are in this field (it sure isn't the pay). We don't actually care if our students become great paddlers or backcountry chefs. What we do care about is that they get something out of their experience that helps them in a future scenario. For example:

> During school one day, Randy gets word of the upcoming nominations for student government. He thinks long and hard about running for class president and wonders if he has what it takes to fill that role. Then, he remembers his experience as leader of the day on his Adventure Education Course. Randy recalls the positive feedback he received from his peers during the debrief, and how he had stated he would no longer be hesitant to seek leadership opportunities. Drawing from this experience, Randy decides to run for class president.

While this is a particularly direct example of transference, we have all had, or will have students, who experience similar situations. It's our job as facilitators to make sure they are thinking about this sort of development during the course, ensuring that these experiences aren't just stand-alone, one-time memories, but that they can have a genuine impact on the lives of our students. This process starts by taking our debriefs one step further and asking follow-up questions to get our students into the mentality that this experience has relevance in their lives, back at home. Some examples of transference questions would be:

1. How is this experience relevant to your life back home?
2. Can you think of similar situations in your daily routine where these learnings might be applicable?
3. How might this experience be useful in your future?
4. What are you going to do differently after this experience?
5. How can you implement this experience into your daily life?

Transference is the key piece of the outdoor adventure teaching that facilitators often miss. Most things that our students learn can actually be generalized to other dimensions of their life and their future. Make sure to emphasize this point. Oftentimes, I'll go so far as to tell my students that this is my objective and that this is what we're striving to do while they are on their course. Additionally, I might consider writing down the things students say in this context, and asking them about it later to emphasize its importance.

Closing the Debrief

Providing a conclusion to your debrief is a critical consideration. You can use this time to provide closure, and summarize any learnings or implications students have discussed. If the debrief discussion has been emotional or heated, providing a clear transition to the next activity will help your students move on. Here are some considerations for closing the debrief:

- Make a "last call" for comments;
- Ask your co-instructor/s if they have anything to add;
- Use a "pregnant pause" to ensure the reluctant-to-speak students have had a chance to express themselves;
- Consider using a quote to articulate or summarize the discussion; and
- Challenge the students to build on the foundation of learning they are creating as you transition to the next activity.

Boosters

The term "boosters" is related to the idea of Post Course Interventions (PCIs) and are used to enhance or encourage the students to recall their experience after the course, off-site. While the benefits of this application are largely unknown, it makes sense to refresh their experience in their minds so that they may remember their course learnings. As facilitators, however, we are faced with a number of issues related to implementing boosters. For example, should you expect to be paid for your efforts to implement a booster? To date, there are few if any organizations that will pay you for your efforts to utilize a booster. There may also be liability concerns, and you should always check with your organization about follow-up procedures with your students.

Boosters are more effective when instructors are more detailed in their teaching. For example, if I write down that a student said she wanted to be more assertive in her communication after the course, I can utilize a booster to provide reminders to hear about this goal as applied in the future. More specifically, I may write a letter or call her on the phone to discuss learnings from the course. The following are some examples of different boosters:

1. <u>Letter to self</u>: Have students write a letter to themselves sometime during the course about things they learned from it that they want to remember. A good time to have them write this letter is while they are alone. Instructors would have them mail the letter at some point after the course;

2. <u>Facebook</u>: Form a Facebook or other social media group that only you and your students have access to after the course. Use this as a place to continue discussions or post questions at certain intervals after the course (i.e. "How have you used the lessons you learned on your course now that you've been back at home for six months?");

3. <u>Skype</u>: We can now create group calls that participants can join and have discussions about their course in a more realistic and visual back and forth;

4. <u>Phone call:</u> Set-up a conference call for you and the students to join into at a given time and day. Facilitate a discussion about how their lives have been different since the course and what they remember from the course.

Write up other booster ideas you might take to follow-up with students:

5. _____

6. _____

7. _____

Although boosters often require facilitators to go beyond the scope of their normal roles, you should definitely try to figure out some way to extend the course for your students and relationships with and between participants beyond the on-course experience. Not only will it be a good reminder for your students, but hopefully it will solidify their experience in their memory and make ongoing contact with other participants a natural process. Additionally, reinforcing the things they learned in this manner might make all the difference in truly changing their lives.

Conclusion

When teaching facilitation, it is good to emphasize that implementing these discussions in a simple manner is the best place to start. You will find your own style, method, and what works best with your personality as you gain experience and receive feedback from students and peers. Remember there is no substitute for experience. Letting your personality and style show in your discussions is often a critical component to having meaningful, in-depth conversations with your students. This, coupled with simply showing them you care about their future, will take you a long way when you facilitate your own experiences. After discussions, get feedback from your co-instructor/s about what worked well for them, or what they might have done differently.

This guide is meant to be a reference and starting point for you to carry along on your courses. Hopefully, you find it useful to reference when you're just starting out or needing to mix up your debriefs on a long course, perhaps because the students are tired of sitting around in a circle and talking at each other. Remember to choose a *trigger*, and then ask them probing questions about their responses to things they have learned. Always facilitate with the end goal that the lessons will carry on and help them in future situations and that indeed, *this is the goal of adventure education*.

When facilitating, remember that facilitating discussions can be therapeutic, but not therapy. If you are interested in providing therapy for student's you need much more training than the Adventure Education field can offer you. Remember that you should never lead student's some place that you're not prepared to take them physically, emotionally, or spiritually.

If this pocket guide enhances even one of your debrief sessions, I consider it worth my time writing it. Thanks, and I hope it helps you enrich the lives of all your students as well as your own work as a facilitator, educator, and mentor.

About the Author

Curt Davidson is a Ph.D. student at Indiana University studying Adventure Education. He has instructed at over eight different Adventure Education Programs including Outward Bound and Summit Adventure. He has also been teaching facilitation in the field and at the university for over seven years. When not on campus, he can be found bumming around the Eastern Sierra or the Cascades of Washington and Oregon where he found the inspiration from fellow instructors and former students for this book.

Acknowledgements

First and foremost, I want to thank the various instructors who I have worked with over the last ten years. Their influences and "tips and tricks" are certainly prevalent in this book, and I am eternally grateful to all of them for their contributions here and in my life. Additionally, I would like to thank Tom Smith for the many discussions that helped lay the foundations for this handbook. Thanks also to Alan Ewert, my friend, mentor, and climbing partner who gave me limitless guidance, both for this book and my life as an instructor and climber. And finally, to my friends and family who make all things I do possible and enjoyable. Hopefully their love and support shows through on these pages because this work is for all of you and in some ways, by all of you.

Field Notes

Field Notes

Field Notes

Facilitation Flow Model

(Quick Reference)

Before

Outcomes pg 8
What outcomes should my students be getting from this experience?

Timing pg 15
Would it be best to debrief right after this activity or let the students process for awhile?

Learning Styles pg 11
What learning styles do I need to cater to during this debrief?

Setting pg 16
Where is the best setting for this that is free from distractions?

During

T - Trigger
R – Recall/Remember
A – Affect/Effect
C - Connection
T - Transference
pg 18

Dynamic Debriefing pg 22
90/10 Rule
Active Listening
Avoid Judgments
Ask follow-up Questions
Take notes

Closing

Closing pg 25
Use a quote or summation to provide a definitive ending or closing on an experience or debrief

Booster pg 26
Consider creating a booster or tangible ways to help the students remember the learning after the experience

10929544R00023

Made in the USA
San Bernardino, CA
02 May 2014